SPOT
WHAT

SPOT WHAT!®

TRAVEL EDITION

hinkler

INTRODUCTION

Spot What!® *Travel Edition* has been created for those of you who enjoy a spotting challenge while on the move. There are over 2000 objects to spot, ranging from simple to challenging, which will keep even the most restless of travelers entertained!

In each picture spread, look at the objects on the right-hand side and see if you can spot them in the scene. You can also read the poem and find the objects listed within the verse.

Once you think you've found everything, try to find the more difficult objects listed in the *Spot What!*® challenges. If you have trouble spotting the objects, use the magnifying glass or check the answers at the end of the book. For more *Spot What!*® fun, play the travel games with friends.

Enjoy travel spotting!

hinkler

Published by Hinkler Pty Ltd
45–55 Fairchild Street
Heatherton Victoria 3202 Australia
www.hinkler.com.au

© Hinkler Pty Ltd 2012, 2014, 2015, 2023

Creators: Nick Bryant and Rowan Summers
Cover design: Peter Tovey
Prepress: Graphic Print Group

Spot What ® registered trade mark number 869534

ISBN: 978 1 7436 7856 5

Printed and manufactured in China

SPOT WHAT! CONTENTS

balloon   wind-up mouse   rocking horse   thimble   abacus   jack   wagon wheel

SPECTACULAR 57

MAGICAL 83

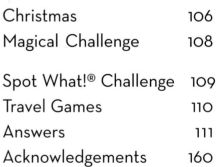

Excalibur   Pan   griffin   voodoo doll   anvil   chameleon   Penny Farthing

Collected things from many lands,
Are stored within a case.
Can you spot two clowns, a coin,
A sad and happy face,

Two ducks, two dogs, two horses,
Two ways of telling time,
Three locks, five eggs, a pumpkin head
And a red stop sign?

cowboy

ball

sun

statue (figurine)

train

shuttlecock

spoon

discus thrower

buffalo

7

Can you spot an egg of green, a white marshmallow, a gum-ball machine,
Two strawberries, a red candy bear, two ice-cream cones, a creamy eclair?
Find two sweet hearts, a car, a muffin, four bananas and three tiny buttons.

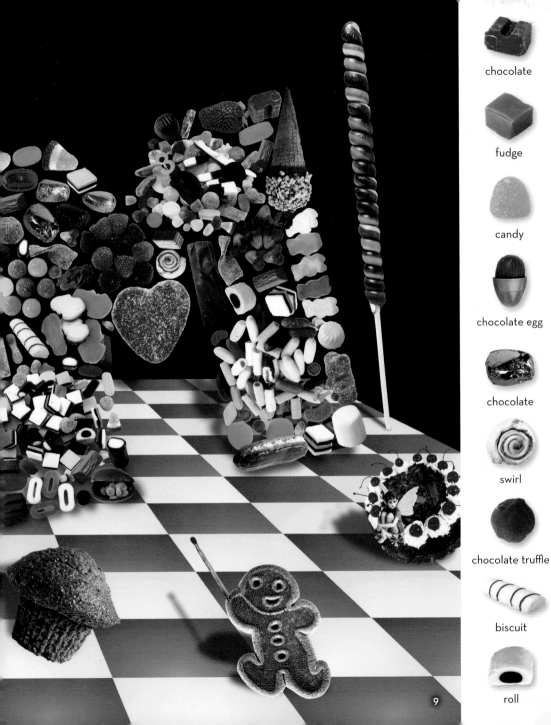

chocolate

fudge

candy

chocolate egg

chocolate

swirl

chocolate truffle

biscuit

roll

9

Can you spot a clown
And a pear,
Four jacks, a thimble
And a bear in a chair?

Can you find a
Tomato face,
A horse's head in
A silly place?

There's a rocket ship,
An owl in a tree
And a way to get
From A to B.

telephone

a die

teddy bear

chair

shield

window

hydrant

flowers

duck

Can you spot five paper clips,
And a Chinese boat,
A rhinoceros, an elephant,
And a mountain goat?

Find the stamp from Musicland,
And a human brain,
A camel and a croissant,
A jet and two biplanes.

binoculars

biplane

boar

croissant

owl

rocket

Santa

shells

tweezers

13

14

Can you spot a cotton reel,
A nib, a tag and a plug,
A yacht, a die, a bolt, a key
And a bright red ladybug?

Can you find three house flies,
A needle and a caterpillar,
Two centipedes, two spiders,
A hook, a nail and a gorilla?

beetle

coin

red ant

hook

nib

paper clip

needle

praying mantis

snail

GORILLA BRAND

SAFETY MATCHES

DO NOT PLAY WITH MATCHES

15

ROOM
TO LET

P →

TELEPHONE

LITTER

Can you spot three arrows,
A window full of clocks,
A tiny little goldfish
And an old mailbox?

Can you find five lemons,
A camera and a cat,
A copy of this page
And a baseball bat?

Can you spot a ship
And a hungry giraffe,
A sign that says FOR SALE,
Three candles in the dark?

1716

DR. MORSE'S
Indian Root Pills

GORDON'S
PIANOS.

sign

camera

bag

seagull

skateboard

trash can

sign

astronaut

Can you spot a wooden plane,
A piano and a house,
A tractor, trike and windmill,
A little wind-up mouse?

Can you find three horses,
A carrot in a truck,
A tambourine, a sewing machine
And a fluffy yellow duck?

toy plane

trike

spaceship

panpipes

bird

panda

dolphin

clock

gypsy

Can you spot a pair
Of scissors,
A wagon wheel and
A shiny mirror,

A pyramid and
A clock,
A dinosaur,
A hose, a sock?

There's a happy ghost,
An old-fashioned hat,
A pair of boots
And a dancing cat.

badge

butterfly

tomato face

Aladdin's lamp

bolt

lamp

Viking helmet

watering can

shell

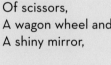

Find a saxophone, a gramophone,
A xylophone, a flute,
Four guitars, three tiny stars,
A golden harp and a lute.

Music makes the world go round,
Seven trumpets can be found,
There's a clarinet, a ukulele too,
They all make wonderful, musical sounds.

musical note

castanets

cello

harmonica

lute

old radio

tambourine

gong

ukulele

The Bank of Smiles

Station Street

Lower Upper Overshot Highway

Lower Upper Overshot Highway

The more you invest in life, the more you get back from it.
A smile costs nothing, but can mean so much.

01/01/2000

To:	Mother Hubbard
Address:	The Shoe
	Nursery Land

LOTS WHIM

Account balance:

1/12/1999	Deposit	12 laughs
	Deposit	17 hugs
	Deposit	34 smiles
	Withdrawal	9 tears

...y most beloved,

How happy I was to ... received your last letter.
...rvellous to read all a... ...to the ...d of
...nds very exciting. ... ...se ...
...en raining here alm... ...this
...arden, but it does m... ...the
...'ve heard that others are going to follow you... to
Mr. Butcher, Mr. Baker and the local Ca... ...n't kn...
all set off to sea in a _tub_ no less. ... ...e that ...
worthiness of such items but I'm ...e that ...as so
I'm sure you will be joining ... ...g as so
W... ...you very much and want
...hearts.

...t the sea

All more lo...

Kuan-Yin

WITH ALL MY LOVE

HAPPY 1st BIRTHDAY

Note

ng List:
~~~es for the dog.
~~ of dog food
~~tle of milk
~~et of dog biscuits
~~le of dog shampoo
Powder
brush

9th

Can you spot a spider,
A medal and a boat,
A telephone, a turtle
And a little love note?

Can you find a bicycle,
A violin and feather,
A map, three green tacks
And five kittens all together?

25

bracelet

dart

knight

paper clip

pencil

scissors

smiley face

sun

elephant

ribbon

bike

ice skates

balloon

lobster

hydrant

drawing pin

guitar

Can you spot
A bus and a train,
A monkey wrench
And a jet plane?

Six strawberries,
Find them all,
A pair of lips
And a ping-pong ball.

Can you find
A big toolbox,
A Christmas hat and
Two Christmas socks?

27

ornament

Can you spot a fisherman,
A peacock and a cat,
A racing horse, a picnic,
A dartboard and a rat?

Can you find the television,
A tower and a gnome,
A little yellow window
And HOME SWEET HOME?

Can you spot a vintage car,
A rabbit and a dog,
A cow, a leaping dolphin
And a little green frog?

camera

polar bear

fish

graveyard

mask

mountain goat

paint palette

spider

windsurfer

29

squid

scraper

boomerang

lizard

The following items are much harder to find, so get ready for the challenge!

CASE (pages 6/7)
2 owls
A musical note
A lizard
2 knights in armor
The Thinker
A Viking ship

YUM (pages 8/9)
A bite
5 bears in a row
2 red twists
The word "HONEY"
2 lollipops
9 balloons

MAZE (pages 10/11)
A rainbow
4 barrels
The words 'SPOT THIS'
The words 'SPOT THAT'
A man with binoculars
3 horned helmets

STAMPS (pages 12/13)
2 leopards
2 stamps from nowhere
A stamp worth 4 peanuts
3 kings
A tiger
A lion

BUGS (pages 14/15)
Butterfly A
Butterfly B
Butterfly C
A knight in armor
A pig
4 clown faces

STREET (pages 16/17)
3 shoes
6 ducks
A lantern
A scary smile
A bonsai garden
A mirror

TOYS (pages 18/19)
2 dinosaurs
An eggbeater
Hammer & wrench
A lion
A purse
The cow that jumped
over the moon

HOUSE (pages 20/21)
7 keys
A fire engine
A skull
A radio
3 chess pieces
A sailing ship

MUSIC (pages 22/23)
A banjo
An accordian
A pair of maracas
A bell
A tin whistle
Bongo drums

PHOTOBOARD (pages 24/25)
9 brass tacks
The words 'HAPPY
BIRTHDAY'
Tic-Tac-Toe
A piano player
A butterfly
A helicopter

RED (pages 26/27)
A tractor
Boltcutters
A hard hat
A feather
A clamp
2 boxing gloves

GALLERY (pages 28/29)
2 carousel horses
A gold teapot
A fork
A wrench
The letters 'OFLCTB'
The words 'THE END'

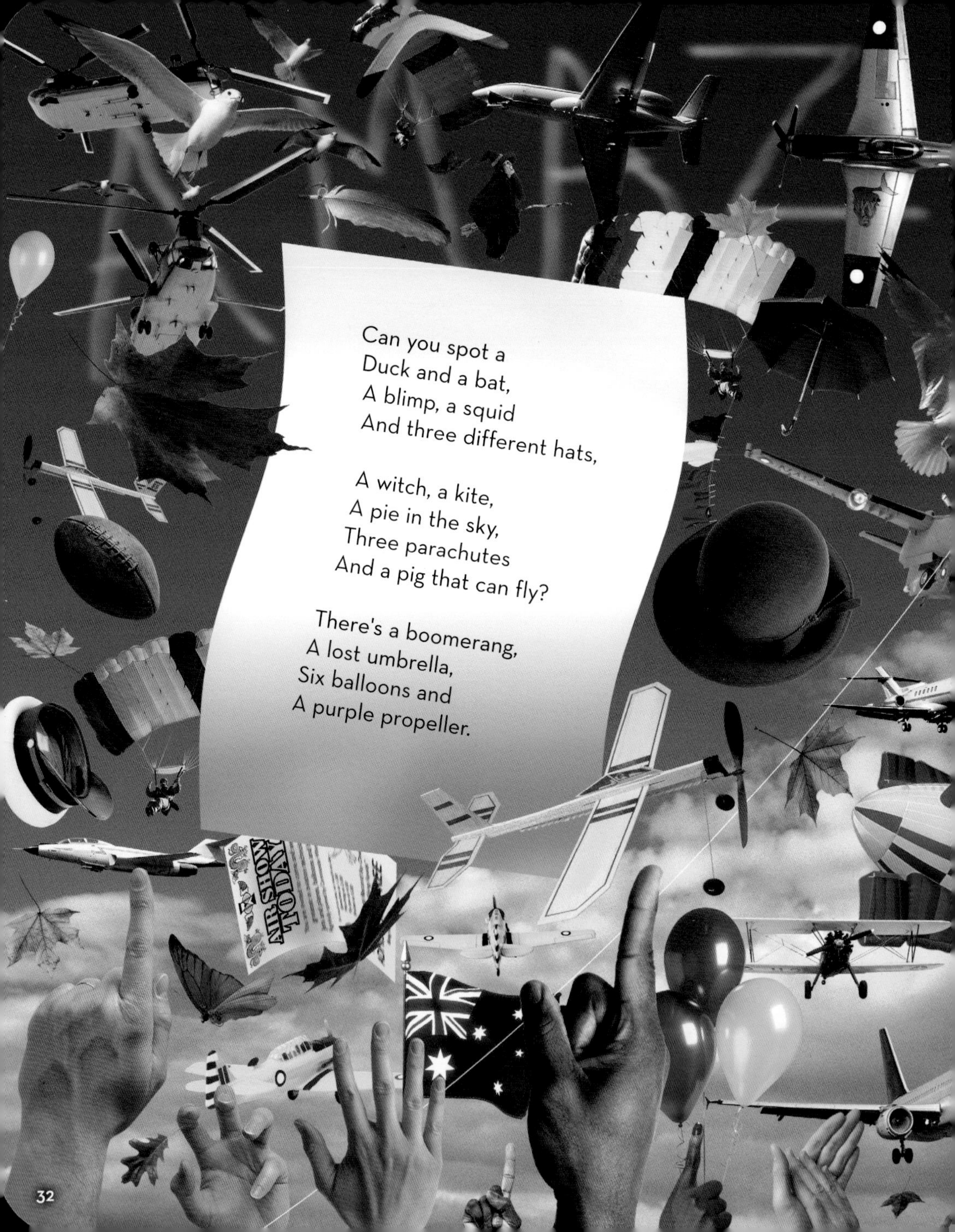

Can you spot a
Duck and a bat,
A blimp, a squid
And three different hats,

A witch, a kite,
A pie in the sky,
Three parachutes
And a pig that can fly?

There's a boomerang,
A lost umbrella,
Six balloons and
A purple propeller.

AIR SHOW TODAY

You are invited to come and see the greatest in aviation technology. Jets and planes, balloons and blimps. Rightfully opened by Commander Whimps (ESQ.)

So much to see, so much to do -
Speeches at 1:00
Marching at 2:00
Fly-bye at 4:00
Rocket at 5:00

"Danger man Dan's" World Record Sky Dive.
Look for the Barn Storming "Flying Squids"

ADMISSION: FREE
Bring the kids.

spotwhat

plane

jet

pie

hand

witch

parrot

football

shuttlecock

blimp

33

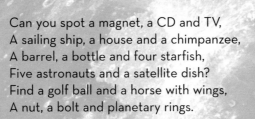

Can you spot a magnet, a CD and TV,
A sailing ship, a house and a chimpanzee,
A barrel, a bottle and four starfish,
Five astronauts and a satellite dish?
Find a golf ball and a horse with wings,
A nut, a bolt and planetary rings.

rubber duck

alien

bottle

badge

red lantern

star

skull

jack

badge

Can you spot an apple core,
A bunch of grapes, a soda can,
Corn on the cob and two hot dogs,
A carrot and a gingerbread man?

Can you find a pizza pie,
Three different types of cheese,
An avocado, half a tomato,
And four little honey bees?

almonds

avocado

broccoli

chick

ice cream

pasta

pear

radish

soda can

Can you spot a pair of pliers,
An axe, a vice, three colored wires,
A hard hat and some plans on paper,
A dripping tap and a scraping scraper?
Find a flashlight, two springs and two locks,
Three paint splats and a red toolbox.

vice

plug

brush

chisel

bolt

hammer

box of nails

plane

bolt

Can you spot a leopard,
A cow, two bulls, two seals,
Two stone cats, a welcome mat,
And three Ferris wheels?

Can you find a baby bear,
A vintage car, a spear,
Five dinosaurs, a clock, a score,
A moose, a sheep, a deer?

knight

balloon

pawn

vintage car

clock

yo-yo

doll

ball

statue

AMAZING FALLS ->

Can you spot a kangaroo,
Five daisies and a snake,
A soccer ball, a pineapple,
A hose, a spade, a rake?

Can you find a squirrel,
A shuttlecock, a gnome,
Three fairies, a canary,
And five pine cones?

flower

butterfly

sunflower

canary

orange flower

frog

hibiscus

hose

rose

Can you spot a bird and a pen,
A telephone and ten after ten,
A truck, a puppet, two buckets, a tie,
A rabbit, a boot and a butterfly?
Find a jukebox, a feather, a star,
A whistle, a flipper, a drum and guitar.

bottle

kittens

clip

present

mouse

vase

paintbrush

stapler

vase

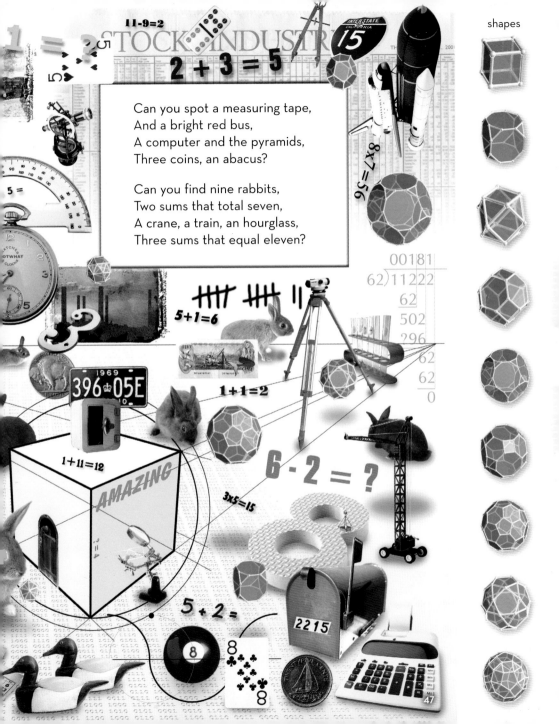

shapes

Can you spot a measuring tape,
And a bright red bus,
A computer and the pyramids,
Three coins, an abacus?

Can you find nine rabbits,
Two sums that total seven,
A crane, a train, an hourglass,
Three sums that equal eleven?

Can you spot a set of keys,
And a red lipstick,
Seven coins, a pack of gum,
And a little candlestick?

Can you spot three brushes,
And a sticky first-aid strip,
Golden wings, five shiny rings,
And a tiny pair of lips?

To you with love

thread

peg

button

brooch

button

pocketknife

thimble

nail clippers

tweezers

Can you spot three dominoes,
Two giraffes and tic-tac-toe,
Three red dice, another blue,
A pawn, a knight and a joker too?
Find eight jacks, a queen, a king,
Two darts, a clown and a yo-yo string.

red ant

Scrabble™ piece

ten of hearts

coin

game piece

lighthouse

coin

gorilla

cannon

SHMONGERS

Next Millennium's Forecast

Strong solar winds

Expected high of 8000 degrees

Night time low...

WEATHER

test signal - please stand by -

bungee jumper

doctor

Spot
Noodle

NEW
EARWAX
FLAVOR

raccoon

remote control

splash

SNEW

17
FUNNEL

tomahawk

Can you spot a goldfish,
An apple and cartoon,
A skier, wolf and tomahawk,
A spider and baboon?

Find a bear, a skunk, a poodle,
And a slide trombone,
A donkey and a lobster,
A watch and microphone.

treadmill

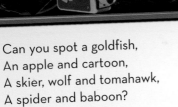

trombone

NEWS
SPOT
WHAT

17

NEWS
WORLD
PEACE

53

WORLD
PEACE

world peace

Can you spot a pumpkin head,
Three balls and a dragon,
Two lizards and a wizard,
And a little red wagon?

Can you find a pair of gloves,
Two orange boots and a frog,
A car, a train, a cowboy,
Three mice, two cats, four dogs?

duck

alarm clock

pogo stick

block

game pieces

gnome

cat

gorilla

moon

solitaire game   nib

AMAZING
SPOT WHAT!®
CHALLENGE

Chinese boat

metronome

The following items are much harder to find, so get ready for the challenge!

FLIGHT (pages 32/33)
A butterfly
4 green leaves
3 hourglasses
An eagle
The world's first plane
A pair of socks
2 elastic bands

ARENA (pages 40/41)
7 jacks
5 barrels
A Native American
A moon
4 shields
The words 'GO GO DANCE'
A path to spell 'AMAZING'

PURSE (pages 48/49)
5 diamonds
A frog
A cat
A pair of scissors
An umbrella
A ticket to Wonderland
A pen

SPACE (pages 34/35)
All 12 zodiac symbols
A parking meter
A picnic
A space shuttle
4 telescopes
Venus and Mars
A kazoo

NATURE (pages 42/43)
A spider
An owl
A hungry bee
A nest
2 lizards
7 snails
A hummingbird

GAMES (pages 50/51)
A fish bowl
A dog
4 flies
A thimble
Solitaire game
A pig
14 marbles

FOOD (pages 36/37)
3 balloons
3 chilli peppers
Some teeth
A Christmas tree
6 airborne peanuts
6 blue candles
6 strawberries

BLUE (pages 44/45)
A typewriter
A seahorse
12 musical notes
4 fish and 3 dolphins
4 boats
4 balls
A rocking chair

MONITORS (pages 52/53)
7 escaped butterflies
A potted plant
A rock band
A door handle
A jack
2 cameras
Headphones

TOOLS (pages 38/39)
5 keys
A needle
3 cogs
3 measuring tools
3 different saws
A microscope
A metronome

NUMBERS (pages 46/47)
The word 'FEBRUARY'
2 boats
3 dominos
A barometer
4 playing cards
The word 'RADAR'
The sun

BEDROOM (pages 54/55)
4 dinosaurs
23 yellow stars
An elephant
6 musical instruments
A fairy
A green plane
7 bears

Can you spot two elephants,
Three giraffes and a bat,
A lion, a tiger, a leopard,
An owl and a pussycat?

Can you find four eagles,
Three dogs, a hippo, a moose,
A sheep, a mouse and a rabbit,
A golden egg and a goose?

SPECTACULAR GORGE

chicken

golden egg

guinea pig

kangaroo

macaw

peacock

polar bears

skunk

turtle

Can you spot a rocking horse,
A piggy-bank, a lollipop,
A sewing machine, a tambourine,
A submarine, a spinning top?

Find a helicopter,
A scarecrow and a bee,
A jack, a train, a crown, a plane,
And the letters 'ABC'.

cat

camera

bird

frying pan

owl

crown

doll

plant

umbrella

Can you spot a birthday cake,
A telephone, a ring,
A rattle and a thimble,
A ladybug, a wing?

Can you find a lobster,
An eyeball and a key,
A skier and an ice cube,
A log, a nest, a tree?

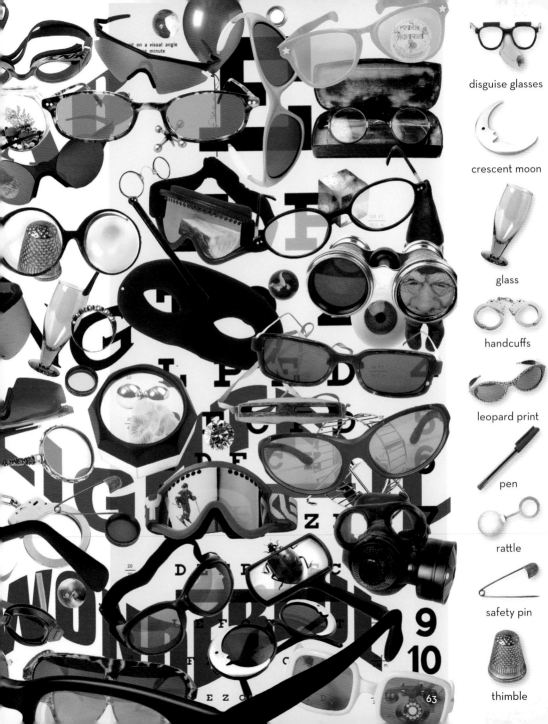

disguise glasses

crescent moon

glass

handcuffs

leopard print

pen

rattle

safety pin

thimble

63

barrel

ornament

traffic light

bird

candy cane

cotton reel

zucchini

glove

chameleon

Can you spot a watering can,
A Christmas tree and a parrot,
A house, a lettuce, an olive,
A chameleon and a carrot?

Find two snakes and a tractor,
A horn and six crawling insects,
Three frogs, a four-leafed clover,
And a Tyrannosaurus rex.

Can you spot a jellyfish,
A seahorse and two skulls,
A turtle and a lighthouse,
One pearl and two seagulls?

Find five leaping dolphins,
A crab, a pair of oars,
An octopus, a treasure chest,
A coin, a kettle, a door.

fish

life jacket

ship

can

windsurfer

bell

gauge

shark

pirate flag

Can you find
A pair of socks,
A stove, a bath,
A flowerbox,

A pump, a nail,
A refrigerator,
A broom, a snail,
And an alligator?

Find five hammers,
Three buckets, a boot,
Two plungers,
Two sponges,
A ladder, a flute.

mop and bucket

spider

plunger

cutters

clamp

wrench

gauge

feather duster

wrench

SPORTING SPECTACULAR

SPOT WHAT

Can you spot a basketball,
A tennis ball, two bats,
A skipping rope, a bowling ball,
A fisherman's hat?

Find a pair of ice skates,
Two whistles and a dart,
A stopwatch, a checkered flag,
A saddle, a horse and cart.

grip exerciser

boxing glove

rollerskates

discus thrower

ball

ticket

cap

baseball

weights

71

Can you find a scorpion,
A lizard and a truck,
A surfboard, a skateboard,
A blackboard and a duck?

Can you spot a windmill,
An astronaut, a car,
An eggshell, a footprint,
A statue, a guitar?

DINGELING BROS.
CIRCUS

Roll Up! Roll Up!,
A spectacular to see,
The circus is in town,
Entertainment guaranteed!

Witness the high-flying
Fellini Brothers,
Perform death-defying,
Stupefying stunts above us,

With jugglers juggling,
Clowns clowning around,
The high wire dare-devils,
Dare-devillings astound,

A better time cannot
Be found anywhere,
So come on down,
To the Circus & Fair

KINDLY CONTROL YOURSELF

Can you spot a juggler,
Five stars and seven clowns,
A trapeze artist, a unicyclist,
A chimp and a merry-go-round,

A pair of tightrope walkers,
Three tumbling acrobats,
An apple, a pear, a balancing chair,
Three hoops and a very tall hat?

SPOT WHAT

cap

bat

pirate hat

bowler hat

hat

fez

mask

crown

teeth

To the Fellini Brothers,

Can you spot a ball of wool,
A stapler and a fan,
A wagon wheel, a fishing reel,
An egg and frying pan?

Find a candelabra,
A knife, a fork and a pie,
A banjo and a compass,
An umbrella and bow tie.

Spectacular Flower Arrangements

10

angel

beaded maraca

candelabra

cup and saucer

dice

fan

baby carriage

pincushion

wagon wheel

PHILOSOPHIÆ
NATURALIS
PRINCIPIA
MATHEMATICA
By
ISAAC NEWTON

Can you spot a wishing well,
A parachute, a polar bear,
A bird in a cage, an open page,
A witch and a rocking chair?

Find a worm and a cuckoo clock,
A brush, a comb and a cello,
Two balloons, a shovel, a spoon,
And five little flowers of yellow.

apple

feather

light bulb

little red wagon

fan

bell

ball

seagull

telescope

Can you spot a jack-in-the-box,
A peacock and a dragon,
A pirate and a rooster,
A ship, a mermaid, a wagon?

Find a hummingbird, a harp,
A unicorn, a kite,
A bucking bronco, a grand piano,
The name of a day and a knight.

SATURDAY

THE
BELL
INN

EAT
AT
JOE'S

THREE LITTLE PIGS
BUILDERS

Blue Snail Couriers
We Get It There Eventually

COMEDY
THEATRE

SPECTACULAR

SPECTACLES

bucking bronco

mouse and cup

train

rose

Pegasus

flying pig

dog

rooster

swan

sundial

joker

SPECTACULAR SPOT WHAT! ® CHALLENGE

candelabra

tuning fork

The following items are much harder to find, so get ready for the challenge!

ANIMALS (pages 58/59)
A frog
3 wise monkeys
3 lizards
2 feathers
Early bird gets worm
A spider and a fly
A snail

BLOCKS (pages 60/61)
9 balloons
A horn
A kettle
5 chess pieces
A piano
A coin
A star

SPECTACLES (pages 62/63)
A diamond
A rhinoceros
A light bulb
A fish bowl
9 marbles
A mirror
A jack

GREEN (pages 64/65)
A circuit board
A leprechaun
Sunglasses
A brussel sprout
A watermelon
A window
10 green bottles

UNDERWATER (pages 66/67)
A catfish and a dogfish
4 starfish
4 scuba divers
A seal
2 anchors
A message in a bottle
7 seashells

PIPES (pages 68/69)
A teapot
5 toilet rolls
An egg
A coat hanger
A fire hydrant
A toilet brush
A set of plans

SPORT (pages 70/71)
A yo-yo
A hockey puck
5 soccer balls
A boomerang
2 catcher's mitts
2 shuttlecocks
2 pairs of binoculars

JIGSAW (pages 72/73)
10 gold bars
A wind-up mouse
A pair of scissors
A jet plane
A London bus
Chinese checkers
A match

CIRCUS (pages 74/75)
2 photographers
3 noisemakers
6 umbrellas
Comedy and Tragedy
2 elephants
A snake
2 elegant penguins

BOUQUET (pages 76/77)
A ship's wheel
An elephant
A gramophone
A fluffy bunny
A pair of ballet shoes
A guitar
A swan

GRAVITY (pages 78/79)
A kitten
A dragonfly
The Mona Lisa
Time flies
East and west
The alphabet
A butter churn

FIREWORKS (pages 80/81)
The Pied Piper
A fish
A bow and arrow
A bridge
A fairy
A skipping girl
A court jester

Can you spot
A candlestick,
An alarm clock,
And a lion,
A frog, a snail,
A puppy dog's tail,
A soldier,
And an iron?

Can you find five
Rubber ducks,
Three mice and a
Gingerbread man,
Three silver bells,
Four cockle shells,
A moon and a
Watering can?

clock

cow and moon

plane

crayon

block

submarine

fish

marker

pinwheel

fishing hook

money

UFO

flashlight

pawn

die

bow tie

sunglasses

bowler hat

Can you spot a bowler hat,
An eggbeater, a toaster,
Two chickens and a cherry,
A piano, a roller coaster?

Can you find a bicycle,
A pencil and a flipper,
Two bubbles and a joker,
A windmill and a zipper?

Can you spot three radios,
A paintbrush and a spring,
An icicle, five vehicles,
A kite, a reel of string?

Can you find a ping-pong ball,
Five flowers and a lock,
A ladybug, three butterflies,
A cactus and a clock?

balloon

flipper

leaf

light bulb

onion

drawing pin

house

wrench

teddy bear

HAPPY BIRTHDAY

JUST MARRIED

141 TAXI

EXIT

89

Can you spot a candy cane,
A pair of pointy shoes,
A heart of gold, a peacock,
An egg and three emus?

Can you find the planet earth,
A clover and two fours,
A car, a boat, a train, a plane,
A sleigh and Santa Claus?

ace of hearts

diamond

ribbon

cup and saucer

present

tickets

four-leaf clover

shooting star

roses

Can you spot a cowboy,
A doctor and a nurse,
Six robots, two teapots,
A parrot and a purse?

Can you find a snowflake,
Someone fast asleep,
A hen, a fox, a jack-in-the-box,
And three of Bo Peep's sheep?

NEXT WEEK THE LILLIPUT AMATEUR TH
presents
MAGICAL MAX AND HIS SU

POPCORN

They're Great!
Moose
BRAND
Nose Plugs

SNOXO
Spot remover
...What works!

ICAL SOCIETY HERE SO..
..ASE OF SORCERY

Just what the Doctor ordered
Plimmsbury's Compound
SMELLS BETTER THAN IT TASTES

Santa

rubber duck

soft toy

frog

doll

balloon

dog

doll

teddy bear

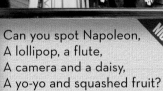

Can you spot Napoleon,
A lollipop, a flute,
A camera and a daisy,
A yo-yo and squashed fruit?

Can you find a saxophone,
A telephone, two crowns,
A tambourine, a flying machine,
A watch, a wand, three clowns?

FOR ONE
NIGHT ONLY

lettuce

Napoleon

toy gun

baseball

rabbit

butterfly

eagle

horn

usher

Can you spot a rhinoceros,
A sheepdog and a shepherd,
A big bad wolf, three little pigs,
A spinning wheel, a leopard?

Can you find three elephants,
A camel and a llama,
A dodo, a stork, an old pitchfork,
Three goats and an iguana?

cleaner

cow

leprechaun

deer

toy soldiers

curtsy

dodo

monk

pumpkin

Can you spot an onion,
A horseshoe and a spoon,
A quill and four chess pieces,
A harp and a bassoon?

Can you find three seashells,
A dogfish and a brain,
A fan, a mortar and pestle,
A lamp and a candle flame?

The Almanac of Handy Hexes

bassoon

coffee grinder

knob

mortar
and pestle

hieroglyphs

brain

pterodactyl

mouse

witch

Can you spot a centaur,
Three skulls, a golden horn,
A scorpion, two griffins,
A witch, a leprechaun?

Find the Loch Ness Monster,
Three unicorns, a key,
A telescope, the pipes of Pan,
A fish, a dove and a bee.

fountain of youth

book

compass

griffin

frog

sundial

dove

pipes of Pan

UFO

mushroom

Can you spot a gargoyle,
Three mirrors and a moose,
A gnome, a coin, a violin,
A shuttlecock, a goose?

Can you find an hourglass,
Two swords and a troll,
A pixie and a pyramid,
A boat and a voodoo doll?

sultan
magic carpets

NEW
SEASON
BROOMS

COMPLETE RANGE OF
TALISMANS

NEW STOCKS
Scrolls &
Parchment

NEW & USED
SPELL
BOOKS
FOR SALE

MAGIC
BEENZ

POTIONS
Freshly
Brewed

FOR
SALE

WANDS
ALL SHAPES
AND SIZES

TROLL

100% PURE
Hobgoblin
ELBOW GREASE

flying carpet

stone crow

dream catcher

helmet

bird

sack of beans

sign

time flies

gargoyle

OCTOBER
31
HALLOWEEN

OCTOBER
30
Saturday

OCTOBER
29
Friday

OCTOBER
28
Thursday

candle

clown

hearse

ice cream

elephant head

toilet roll

doctor

vampire

vulture

Can you spot a wagon wheel,
A rooster and a crow,
A pirate and three apples,
Two ghosts and a wheelbarrow?

Can you find the invisible man,
Two sacks, an axe, a skunk,
A hearse, a horse, a haunted house,
Three witches' hats and a trunk?

FOR SALE

SHEE'S APPLES

Can you spot two reindeer,
Two penguins and a bear,
A letterbox, three pine cones,
A fireplace and a chair?

Can you find a snowman,
A puppy and four cars,
A sailboat and a dinosaur,
Two tops and two guitars?

dice

flamingo

golf clubs

gramophone

ice sculpture

lighthouse

motorbike

piano

top

gargoyle

Napoleon

MAGICAL
SPOT WHAT!®
CHALLENGE

flying
machine

obelisk

The following items are much harder to find, so get ready for the challenge!

IMAGINE (pages 84/85)
A heart
6 paper planes
An apple
A golden egg
An abacus
Fl 130
A family

MAGIC (pages 86/87)
A domino
A boomerang
A canoe
A nut and bolt
A light bulb
2 keys
An eye spying

RAINBOW (pages 88/89)
A bee
5 telephones
2 snakes
A pair of gloves
2 drums
A funnel
2 pairs of scissors

WISH (pages 90/91)
A winning hand
A bride and groom
7 pots of gold
A pineapple
An arched window
2 Christmas trees
A rabbit

AUDIENCE (pages 92/93)
A snake
Sunglasses
A soccer ball
A volley ball
A football
A tennis ball
Knitting

STAGE (pages 94/95)
A set of keys
A puffin
A vase
A penny farthing
A torch
A pen
A banana peel

CASTLE (pages 96/97)
Rapunzel
3 kings
A rooster
A mousetrap
Quasimodo
A pocket watch
A pirate flag

LABORATORY (pages 98/99)
A centaur
The solar system
A chocolate frog
A goose
2 butterflies
A coffee mug
An umbrella

MYTHS (pages 100/101)
The sun
The tooth fairy
Excalibur
The magic harp
A woodpecker
An obelisk
A tall ship

EMPORIUM (pages 102/103)
A saw
A hammer
A pair of pliers
A clamp
2 axes
A dart
3 wands

HALLOWEEN (pages 104/105)
Headless horseman
2 candelabras
A cowardly lion
3 lanterns
2 pumpkin pies
An oilcan
9 skulls

CHRISTMAS (pages 106/107)
2 gingerbread men
3 snowflakes
5 sleds
A pogo stick
A woolly mitten
A birdhouse
Spectacles

SPOT WHAT!® CHALLENGE

Did you notice that some things appear more than once?
Can you find the words 'SPOT WHAT' in every picture?

lobster

In **PICTURE HUNT** can you find:

A fairy and a three,
A matchstick, an apple
And a honey bee?

discus thrower

---

pinwheel

In **AMAZING** can you find:

A mermaid and a four,
A ladybug, a light bulb,
And a little blue door?

UFO

---

grip exerciser

In **SPECTACULAR** can you find:

The number ten, a gnome,
A butterfly, an hourglass,
And an ice-cream cone?

plane

---

curtsy

In **MAGICAL** can you find:

A crystal ball, a cat,
A knight, a dragon, a wizard,
An owl and a black top hat?

DOWN WITH
PRINCE
CHARMING

monk

SPOT WHAT! TRAVEL GAMES

CALL AND SPOT

1. The oldest player goes first.

2. He or she is 'the caller' and the other player is 'the spotter'. The caller chooses a page from the book and picks an item for the spotter to find, saying, for example, 'Can you spot a boomerang?'

3. The spotter must then try to find the item.

4. If the spotter can't find it, the caller gets 5 points and shows the spotter where it is and has another turn.

5. If the spotter can find the item, then he or she gets 5 points and now it's his or her turn to be the caller.

6. The first to reach 30 points wins but you could also set your own limit or simply play best out of three!

7. You can make the game more challenging by putting a time limit of one to three minutes on each search.

SPOT AND RHYME

1. The youngest player goes first.

2. He or she is 'the spotter' and the other player is 'the poet'. The spotter finds six items for the poet to use in a poem.

3. The poet then creates a four-lined poem making sure the end of the 2nd line rhymes with the end of the 4th line. For example, 'dog' rhymes with 'frog' in this poem:

> Can you spot a vintage car,
> A rabbit and a dog,
> A cow, a leaping dolphin
> And a little green frog?

4. Once a poem is created, the poet switches roles with the spotter.

5. You can make the game more challenging by increasing or decreasing the number of items to use in a poem.

ice skates

dog

vintage car

knight

gramophone

old radio

dancing cat

CASE (pages 6–7)

Blue circles indicate objects listed in the poem and on the right side of the page.
Pink circles indicate objects listed in the *Spot What!®* challenges.

Collected things from many lands,
Are stored within a case.
Can you spot two clowns, a coin,
A sad and happy face,

Two ducks, two dogs, two horses,
Two ways of telling time,
Three locks, five eggs, a pumpkin head
And a red stop sign?

YUM (pages 8-9)

Can you spot an egg of green, a white marshmallow, a gum-ball machine,
Two strawberries, a red candy bear, two ice-cream cones, a creamy eclair?
Find two sweet hearts, a car, a muffin, four bananas and three tiny buttons.

ANSWERS: PICURE HUNT

MAZE (pages 10–11)

Blue circles indicate objects listed in the poem and on the right side of the page.
Pink circles indicate objects listed in the *Spot What!®* challenges.

Can you spot a clown
And a pear,
Four jacks, a thimble,
And a bear in a chair?

Can you find a
Tomato face,
A horse's head in
A silly place?

There's a rocket ship,
An owl in a tree
And a way to get
From A to B.

STAMPS (pages 12–13)

Blue circles indicate objects listed in the poem and on the right side of the page.
Pink circles indicate objects listed in the *Spot What!*® challenges.

Can you spot five paper clips,
And a Chinese boat,
A rhinoceros, an elephant,
And a mountain goat?

Find the stamp from Musicland,
And a human brain,
A camel and a croissant,
A jet and two biplanes.

BUGS (pages 14–15)

Blue circles indicate objects listed in the poem and on the right side of the page.
Pink circles indicate objects listed in the Spot What!® challenges.

Can you spot a cotton reel,
A nib, a tag and a plug,
A yacht, a die, a bolt, a key
And a bright red ladybug?

Can you find three house flies,
A needle and a caterpillar,
Two centipedes, two spiders,
A hook, a nail and a gorilla?

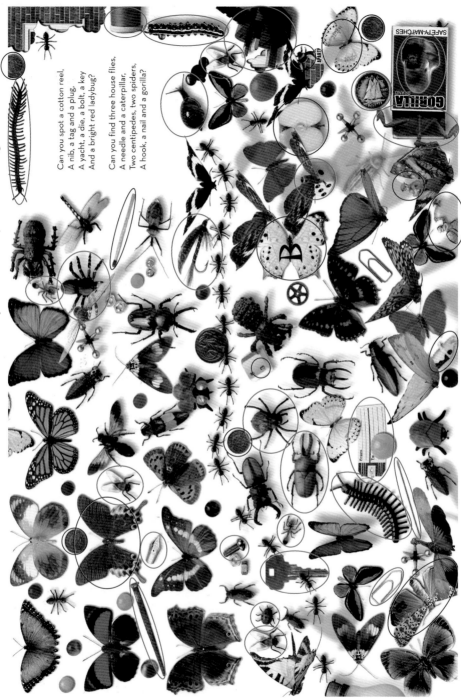

STREET (pages 16–17)

Blue circles indicate objects listed in the poem and on the right side of the page.
Pink circles indicate objects listed in the *Spot What!®* challenges.

Can you spot three arrows,
A window full of clocks,
A tiny little goldfish
And an old mailbox?

Can you find five lemons,
A camera and a cat,
A copy of this page
And a baseball bat?

Can you spot a ship,
And a hungry giraffe,
A sign that says FOR SALE,
Three candles in the dark?

TOYS (pages 18–19)

Blue circles indicate objects listed in the poem and on the right side of the page.
Pink circles indicate objects listed in the *Spot What!®* challenges.

Can you spot a wooden plane,
A piano and a house,
A tractor, trike and windmill,
A little wind-up mouse?

Can you find three horses,
A carrot in a truck,
A tambourine, a sewing machine
And a fluffy yellow duck?

HOUSE (pages 20–21)

Blue circles indicate objects listed in the poem and on the right side of the page.
Pink circles indicate objects listed in the *Spot What!®* challenges.

Can you spot a pair
Of scissors,
A wagon wheel and
A shiny mirror,

A pyramid and
A clock,
A dinosaur,
A hose, a sock?

There's a happy ghost,
An old-fashioned hat,
A pair of boots
And a dancing cat.

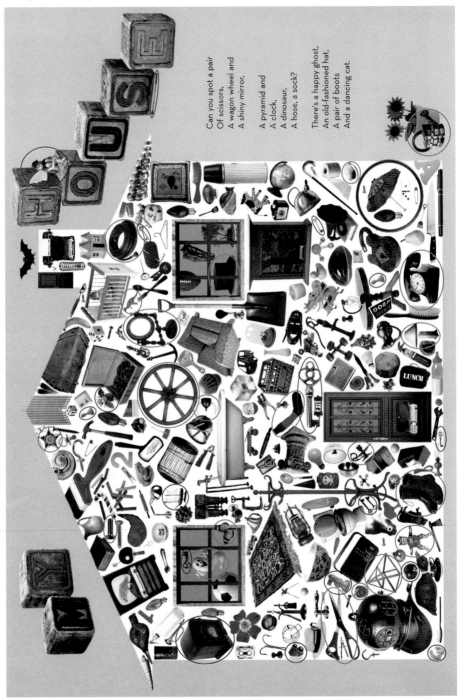

MUSIC (pages 22–23)

Blue circles indicate objects listed in the poem and on the right side of the page.
Pink circles indicate objects listed in the *Spot What!®* challenges.

Find a saxophone, a gramophone,
A xylophone, a flute,
Four guitars, three tiny stars,
A golden harp and a lute.

Music makes the world go round,
Seven trumpets can be found,
There's a clarinet, a ukulele too,
They all make wonderful, musical sounds.

PHOTOBOARD (pages 24–25)

Blue circles indicate objects listed in the poem and on the right side of the page.
Pink circles indicate objects listed in the *Spot What!®* challenges.

RED (pages 26–27)

Blue circles indicate objects listed in the poem and on the right side of the page.
Pink circles indicate objects listed in the *Spot What!®* challenges.

Can you spot
A bus and a train,
A monkey wrench
And a jet plane?

Six strawberries,
Find them all,
A pair of lips
And a ping-pong ball.

Can you find
A big toolbox,
A Christmas hat and
Two Christmas socks?

GALLERY (pages 28–29)

Blue circles indicate objects listed in the poem and on the right side of the page.
Pink circles indicate objects listed in the *Spot What!®* challenges.

Can you spot a fisherman,
A peacock and a cat,
A racing horse, a picnic,
A dartboard and a rat?

Can you find the television,
A tower and a gnome,
A little yellow window
And HOME SWEET HOME?

Can you spot a vintage car,
A rabbit and a dog,
A cow, a leaping dolphin
And a little green frog?

FLIGHT (pages 32-33)

Blue circles indicate objects listed in the poem and on the right side of the page.
Pink circles indicate objects listed in the *Spot What!*® challenges.

Can you spot a
Duck and a bat,
A blimp, a squid
And three different hats,

A witch, a kite,
A pie in the sky,
Three parachutes
And a pig that can fly?

There's a boomerang,
A lost umbrella,
Six balloons and
A purple propeller.

Blue circles indicate objects listed in the poem and on the right side of the page.
Pink circles indicate objects listed in the Spot What!® challenges.

Can you spot a magnet, a CD and TV,
A sailing ship, a house and a chimpanzee,
A barrel, a bottle and four starfish,
Five astronauts and a satellite dish?
Find a golf ball and a horse with wings,
A nut, a bolt and planetary rings.

ANSWERS: **AMAZING**

FOOD (pages 36–37)

Blue circles indicate objects listed in the poem and on the right side of the page.
Pink circles indicate objects listed in the *Spot What!* challenges.

Can you spot an apple core,
A bunch of grapes, a soda can,
Corn on the cob and two hot dogs,
A carrot and a gingerbread man?

Can you find a pizza pie,
Three different types of cheese,
An avocado, half a tomato,
And four little honey bees?

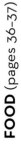

TOOLS (pages 38–39)

Blue circles indicate objects listed in the poem and on the right side of the page.
Pink circles indicate objects listed in the Spot What!® challenges.

Can you spot a pair of pliers,
An axe, a vice, three colored wires,
A hard hat and some plans on paper,
A dripping tap and a scraping scraper?
Find a flashlight, two springs and two locks,
Three paint splats and a red toolbox.

ARENA (pages 40–41)

Blue circles indicate objects listed in the poem and on the right side of the page.
Pink circles indicate objects listed in the Spot What! challenges.

Can you spot a leopard,
A cow, two bulls, two seals,
Two stone cats, a welcome mat,
And three Ferris wheels?

Can you find a baby bear,
A vintage car, a spear,
Five dinosaurs, a clock, a score,
A moose, a sheep, a deer?

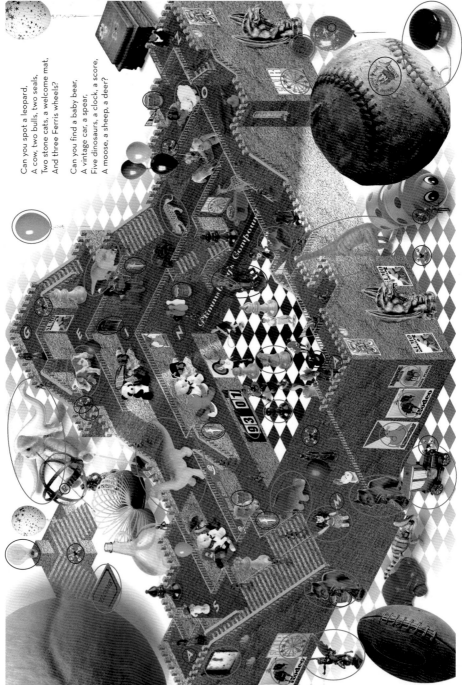

NATURE (pages 42–43)

Blue circles indicate objects listed in the poem and on the right side of the page.
Pink circles indicate objects listed in the *Spot What!®* challenges.

Can you spot a kangaroo,
Five daisies and a snake,
A soccer ball, a pineapple,
A hose, a spade, a rake?

Can you find a squirrel,
A shuttlecock, a gnome,
Three fairies, a canary,
And five pine cones?

AMAZING FALLS →

BLUE (pages 44–45)

Blue circles indicate objects listed in the poem and on the right side of the page.
Pink circles indicate objects listed in the *Spot What!®* challenges.

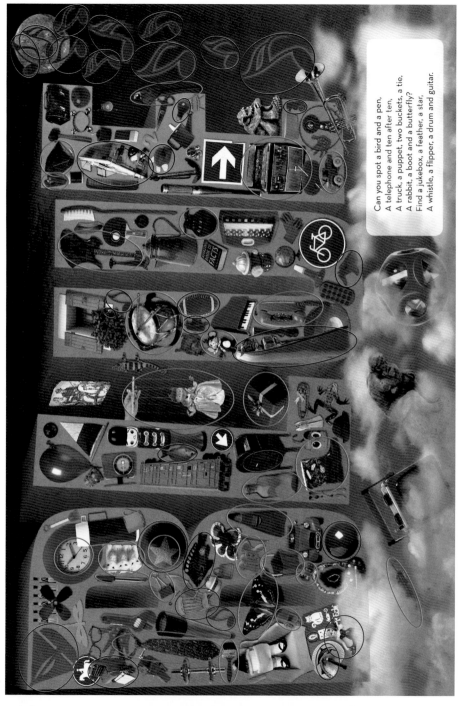

Can you spot a bird and a pen,
A telephone and ten after ten,
A truck, a puppet, two buckets, a tie,
A rabbit, a boot and a butterfly?
Find a jukebox, a feather, a star,
A whistle, a flipper, a drum and guitar.

NUMBERS (pages 46–47)

Blue circles indicate objects listed in the poem and on the right side of the page.
Pink circles indicate objects listed in the *Spot What!*® challenges.

Can you spot a measuring tape,
And a bright red bus,
A computer and the pyramids,
Three coins, an abacus?

Can you find nine rabbits,
Two sums that total seven,
A crane, a train, an hourglass,
Three sums that equal eleven?

PURUSE (pages 48–49)

Blue circles indicate objects listed in the poem and on the right side of the page.
Pink circles indicate objects listed in the *Spot What!* challenges.

Can you spot a set of keys,
And a red lipstick,
Seven coins, a pack of gum,
And a little candlestick?

Can you spot three brushes,
And a sticky first-aid strip,
Golden wings, five shiny rings,
And a tiny pair of lips?

To you with love

GAMES (pages 50–51)

Can you spot three dominoes,
Two giraffes and tic-tac-toe,
Three red dice, another blue,
A pawn, a knight and a joker too?
Find eight jacks, a queen, a king,
Two darts, a clown and a yo-yo string.

Blue circles indicate objects listed in the poem and on the right side of the page.
Pink circles indicate objects listed in the *Spot What!* challenges.

MONITORS (pages 52–53)

Blue circles indicate objects listed in the poem and on the right side of the page.
Pink circles indicate objects listed in the *Spot What!®* challenges.

Can you spot a goldfish,
An apple and cartoon,
A skier, wolf and tomahawk,
A spider and baboon?

Find a bear, a skunk, a poodle,
And a slide trombone,
A donkey and a lobster,
A watch and microphone.

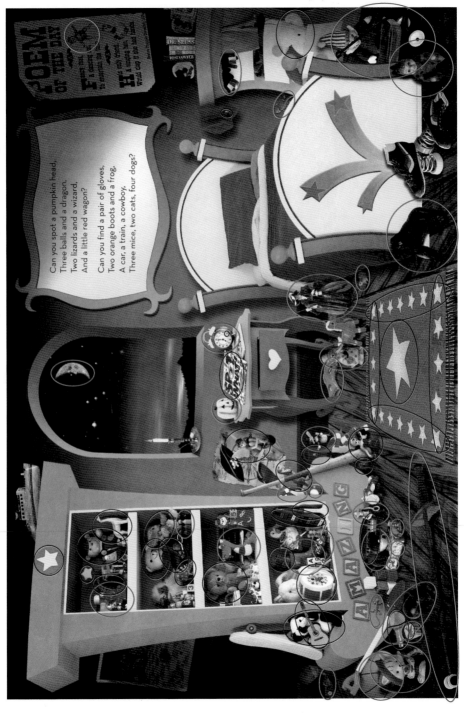

BEDROOM (pages 54–55)

Blue circles indicate objects listed in the poem and on the right side of the page.
Pink circles indicate objects listed in the *Spot What!* challenges.

Can you spot a pumpkin head,
Three balls and a dragon.
Two lizards and a wizard.
And a little red wagon?

Can you find a pair of gloves,
Two orange boots and a frog,
A car, a train, a cowboy,
Three mice, two cats, four dogs?

ANIMALS (pages 58–59)

Blue circles indicate objects listed in the poem and on the right side of the page.
Pink circles indicate objects listed in the *Spot What!* challenges.

Can you spot two elephants,
Three giraffes and a bat,
A lion, a tiger, a leopard,
An owl and a pussycat?

Can you find four eagles,
Three dogs, a hippo, a moose,
A sheep, a mouse and a rabbit,
A golden egg and a goose?

BLOCKS (pages 60–61)

Blue circles indicate objects listed in the poem and on the right side of the page.
Pink circles indicate objects listed in the *Spot What!*® challenges.

Can you spot a rocking horse,
A piggy-bank, a lollipop,
A sewing machine, a tambourine,
A submarine, a spinning top?

Find a helicopter,
A scarecrow and a bee,
A jack, a train, a crown, a plane,
And the letters 'ABC'.

ANSWERS: **SPECTACULAR**

SPECTACLES (pages 62–63)

Blue circles indicate objects listed in the poem and on the right side of the page.
Pink circles indicate objects listed in the *Spot What!*® challenges.

Can you spot a birthday cake,
A telephone, a ring,
A rattle and a thimble,
A ladybug, a wing?

Can you find a lobster,
An eyeball and a key,
A skier and an ice cube,
A log, a nest, a tree?

Blue circles indicate objects listed in the poem and on the right side of the page.
Pink circles indicate objects listed in the *Spot What!®* challenges.

Can you spot a watering can,
A Christmas tree and a parrot,
A house, a lettuce, an olive,
A chameleon and a carrot?

Find two snakes and a tractor,
A horn and six crawling insects,
Three frogs, a four-leafed clover,
And a Tyrannosaurus rex.

FREEWAY ENTRANCE

UNDERWATER (pages 66-67)

Blue circles indicate objects listed in the poem and on the right side of the page.
Pink circles indicate objects listed in the *Spot What!®* challenges.

Can you spot a jellyfish,
A seahorse and two skulls,
A turtle and a lighthouse,
One pearl and two seagulls?

Find five leaping dolphins,
A crab, a pair of oars,
An octopus, a treasure chest,
A coin, a kettle, a door.

PIPES (pages 68–69)

Blue circles indicate objects listed in the poem and on the right side of the page.
Pink circles indicate objects listed in the *Spot What!®* challenges.

Can you find
A pair of socks,
A stove, a bath,
A flowerbox,

A pump, a nail,
A refrigerator,
A broom, a snail,
And an alligator?

Find five hammers,
Three buckets, a boot,
Two plungers,
Two sponges,
A ladder, a flute.

Blue circles indicate objects listed in the poem and on the right side of the page.
Pink circles indicate objects listed in the *Spot What!®* challenges.

Can you spot a basketball,
A tennis ball, two bats,
A skipping rope, a bowling ball,
A fisherman's hat?

Find a pair of ice skates,
Two whistles and a dart,
A stopwatch, a checkered flag,
A saddle, a horse and cart.

JIGSAW (pages 72-73)

Blue circles indicate objects listed in the poem and on the right side of the page.
Pink circles indicate objects listed in the *Spot What!®* challenges.

Can you find a scorpion,
A lizard and a truck,
A surfboard, a skateboard,
A blackboard and a duck?

Can you spot a windmill,
An astronaut, a car,
An eggshell, a footprint,
A statue, a guitar?

CIRCUS (pages 74–75)

Blue circles indicate objects listed in the poem and on the right side of the page.
Pink circles indicate objects listed in the *Spot What!®* challenges.

Can you spot a juggler,
Five stars and seven clowns,
A trapeze artist, a unicyclist,
A chimp and a merry-go-round,

A pair of tightrope walkers,
Three tumbling acrobats,
An apple, a pear, a balancing chair,
Three hoops and a very tall hat?

BOUQUET (pages 76–77)

Blue circles indicate objects listed in the poem and on the right side of the page.
Pink circles indicate objects listed in the Spot What!® challenges.

Spectacular Flower Arrangements

To the Fellini Brothers,

Can you spot a ball of wool,
A stapler and a fan,
A wagon wheel, a fishing reel,
An egg and frying pan?

Find a candelabra,
A knife, a fork and a pie,
A banjo and a compass,
An umbrella and bow tie.

GRAVITY (pages 78-79)

Blue circles indicate objects listed in the poem and on the right side of the page.
Pink circles indicate objects listed in the *Spot What!®* challenges.

Can you spot a wishing well,
A parachute, a polar bear,
A bird in a cage, an open page,
A witch and a rocking chair?

Find a worm and a cuckoo clock,
A brush, a comb and a cello,
Two balloons, a shovel, a spoon,
And five little flowers of yellow.

FIREWORKS (pages 80–81)

Blue circles indicate objects listed in the poem and on the right side of the page.
Pink circles indicate objects listed in the Spot What!® challenges.

Can you spot a jack-in-the-box,
A peacock and a dragon,
A pirate and a rooster,
A ship, a mermaid, a wagon?

Find a hummingbird, a harp,
A unicorn, a kite,
A bucking bronco, a grand piano,
The name of a day and a knight.

IMAGE (pages 84–85)

Blue circles indicate objects listed in the poem and on the right side of the page.
Pink circles indicate objects listed in the *Spot What!®* challenges.

Can you spot
A candlestick,
An alarm clock,
And a lion,
A frog, a snail,
A puppy dog's tail,
A soldier,
And an iron?

Can you find five
Rubber ducks,
Three mice and a
Gingerbread man,
Three silver bells,
Four cockle shells,
A moon and a
Watering can?

Blue circles indicate objects listed in the poem and on the right side of the page.
Pink circles indicate objects listed in the *Spot What!* challenges.

Can you spot a bowler hat,
An eggbeater, a toaster,
Two chickens and a cherry,
A piano, a roller coaster?

Can you find a bicycle,
A pencil and a flipper,
Two bubbles and a joker,
A windmill and a zipper?

ANSWERS: **MAGICAL**

RAINBOW (pages 88–89)

Blue circles indicate objects listed in the poem and on the right side of the page.
Pink circles indicate objects listed in the *Spot What!®* challenges.

Can you spot three radios,
A paintbrush and a spring,
An icicle, five vehicles,
A kite, a reel of string?

Can you find a ping-pong ball,
Five flowers and a lock,
A ladybug, three butterflies,
A cactus and a clock?

WISH (pages 90–91)

Blue circles indicate objects listed in the poem and on the right side of the page.
Pink circles indicate objects listed in the Spot What!® challenges.

Can you spot a candy cane,
A pair of pointy shoes,
A heart of gold, a peacock,
An egg and three emus?

Can you find the planet earth,
A clover and two fours,
A car, a boat, a train, a plane,
A sleigh and Santa Claus?

AUDIENCE (pages 92–93)

Blue circles indicate objects listed in the poem and on the right side of the page.
Pink circles indicate objects listed in the *Spot What!®* challenges.

Program

Can you spot a cowboy,
A doctor and a nurse,
Six robots, two teapots,
A parrot and a purse?

Can you find a snowflake,
Someone fast asleep,
A hen, a fox, a jack-in-the-box,
And three of Bo Peep's sheep?

STAGE (pages 94–95)

Blue circles indicate objects listed in the poem and on the right side of the page.
Pink circles indicate objects listed in the *Spot What!* challenges.

FOR ONE NIGHT ONLY

Can you spot Napoleon,
A lollipop, a flute,
A camera and a daisy,
A yo-yo and squashed fruit?

Can you find a saxophone,
A telephone, two crowns,
A tambourine, a flying machine,
A watch, a wand, three clowns?

CASTLE (pages 96–97)

Blue circles indicate objects listed in the poem and on the right side of the page.
Pink circles indicate objects listed in the *Spot What!*® challenges.

Can you spot a rhinoceros,
A sheepdog and a shepherd,
A big bad wolf, three little pigs,
A spinning wheel, a leopard?

Can you find three elephants,
A camel and a llama,
A dodo, a stork, an old pitchfork,
Three goats and an iguana?

Blue circles indicate objects listed in the poem and on the right side of the page.
Pink circles indicate objects listed in the *Spot What!®* challenges.

Can you spot an onion,
A horseshoe and a spoon,
A quill and four chess pieces,
A harp and a bassoon?

Can you find three seashells,
A dogfish and a brain,
A fan, a mortar and pestle,
A lamp and a candle flame?

MYTHS (pages 100–101)

Can you spot a centaur,
Three skulls, a golden horn,
A scorpion, two griffins,
A witch, a leprechaun?

Find the Loch Ness Monster,
Three unicorns, a key,
A telescope, the pipes of Pan,
A fish, a dove and a bee.

Blue circles indicate objects listed in the poem and on the right side of the page.
Pink circles indicate objects listed in the *Spot What!®* challenges.

EMPORIUM (pages 102–103)

Blue circles indicate objects listed in the poem and on the right side of the page.
Pink circles indicate objects listed in the *Spot What!®* challenges.

Can you spot a gargoyle,
Three mirrors and a moose,
A gnome, a coin, a violin,
A shuttlecock, a goose?

Can you find an hourglass,
Two swords and a troll,
A pixie and a pyramid,
A boat and a voodoo doll?

HALLOWEEN (pages 104–105)

Blue circles indicate objects listed in the poem and on the right side of the page.
Pink circles indicate objects listed in the *Spot What!*® challenges.

Can you spot a wagon wheel,
A rooster and a crow,
A pirate and three apples,
Two ghosts and a wheelbarrow?

Can you find the invisible man,
Two sacks, an axe, a skunk,
A hearse, a horse, a haunted house,
Three witches' hats and a trunk?

CHRISTMAS (pages 106–107)

Blue circles indicate objects listed in the poem and on the right side of the page.
Pink circles indicate objects listed in the *Spot What!®* challenges.

Can you spot two reindeer,
Two penguins and a bear,
A letterbox, three pine cones,
A fireplace and a chair?

Can you find a snowman,
A puppy and four cars,
A sailboat and a dinosaur,
Two tops and two guitars?

WELCOME TO THE
NORTH POLE

ACKNOWLEDGEMENTS

We would like to thank the following people:

barometer

The Thinker

Sam Grimmer
Peter Wakeman
Peter Tovey Studios
Kate Bryant
Paul Scott
TommyZ
Toby Bishop
Kristie Maxwell
Kelly-Anne Thompson
Miles Summers
Ruth Coleman
Heather Hammonds
Christopher Timms
Gillian Banham

Helena Newton
Sam Bryant
Suzanne Buckley
Claire Tennant
Dingeling Bros Circus
Samantha Boardman
Kendra Bishop
Derek Debenham
Rod and Mary Bryant
Louise Coulthard
Silvana Paolini
Stephen Ungar
Stephen Bishop
Kendra Bishop

Graphic Print Group
Albert Meli from Continuous Recall
Oi Crystals Fossils Minerals, Melbourne, Vic
Little Ashlie, Michael, Nicole and James, for lending their toys
Everyone at Hinkler Books

Backgrounds for Gravity, Circus, Castle, Stage, Audience, and Emporium
by Stephen Evans s_evans42@yahoo.com
Furniture for 'Bedroom' created by Christopher Peregrine Timms
www.christophertimms.com.au
Thanks to Tsutomu Higo for the use of geometric models for 'Numbers'
www.asahi-net.or.jp/-nj2t-hg/

telephone

mortar and pestle

king

emu

spinning wheel

Big Bad Wolf

hourglass